DOODLE GIRLS
Coloring Book for Adults

ZenMaster Coloring Books

Helpful Tips for Coloring

~ Sometimes the colors appear differently on paper than what you would expect. Use the color test page to play with your colors beforehand.

~ If you are using colored pencils make sure to keep them sharp. This helps when coloring smaller areas or details on the page. Fine point sharpies also work great for smaller areas.

~ Speaking of sharpies, make sure you put a scrap piece of paper behind the page you are coloring to keep the markers from bleeding to the next page.

~ When using crayons or pencils start out light. You can always go back and darken later.

~ There are so many tools for coloring: markers, sharpies, crayons, pencils, pastels, and the list goes on. Experiment with what works best for you and your designs. Though it's not necessary, using higher quality coloring utensils makes a difference.

~ If you come to a design that seems overwhelming just pick a place to start and go from there. Once you begin your creativity will quickly take over!! If you get discouraged just take a break and come back to the page later.

~ Remember to practice. Like anything else, the more you do it the better you'll get. It'll become more and more relaxing each time.

~ DON'T FOLLOW THE RULES! It's up to you how you color your designs. Just let your creativity take the lead and HAVE FUN!

COLOR TEST PAGE

COLOR TEST PAGE

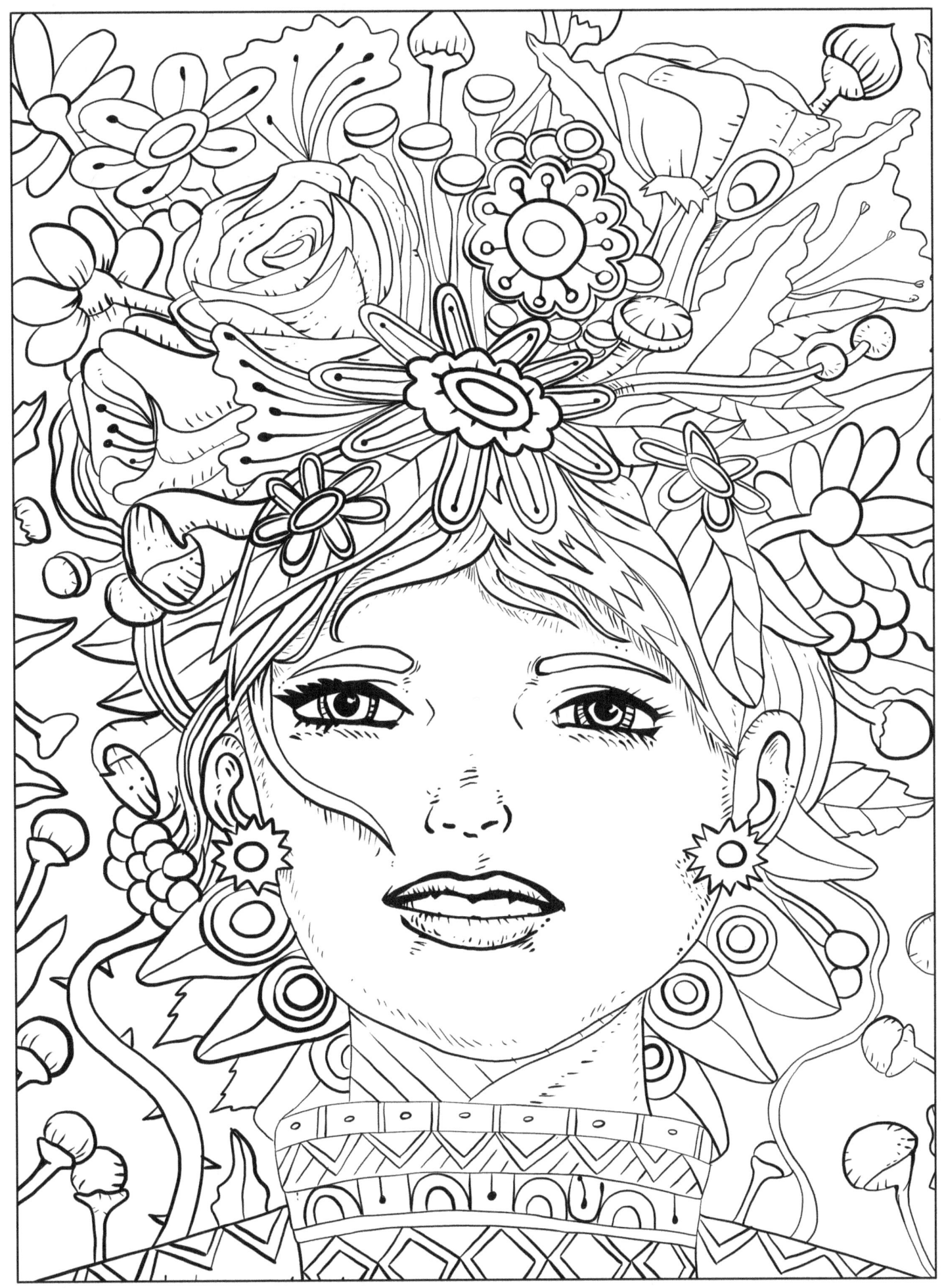

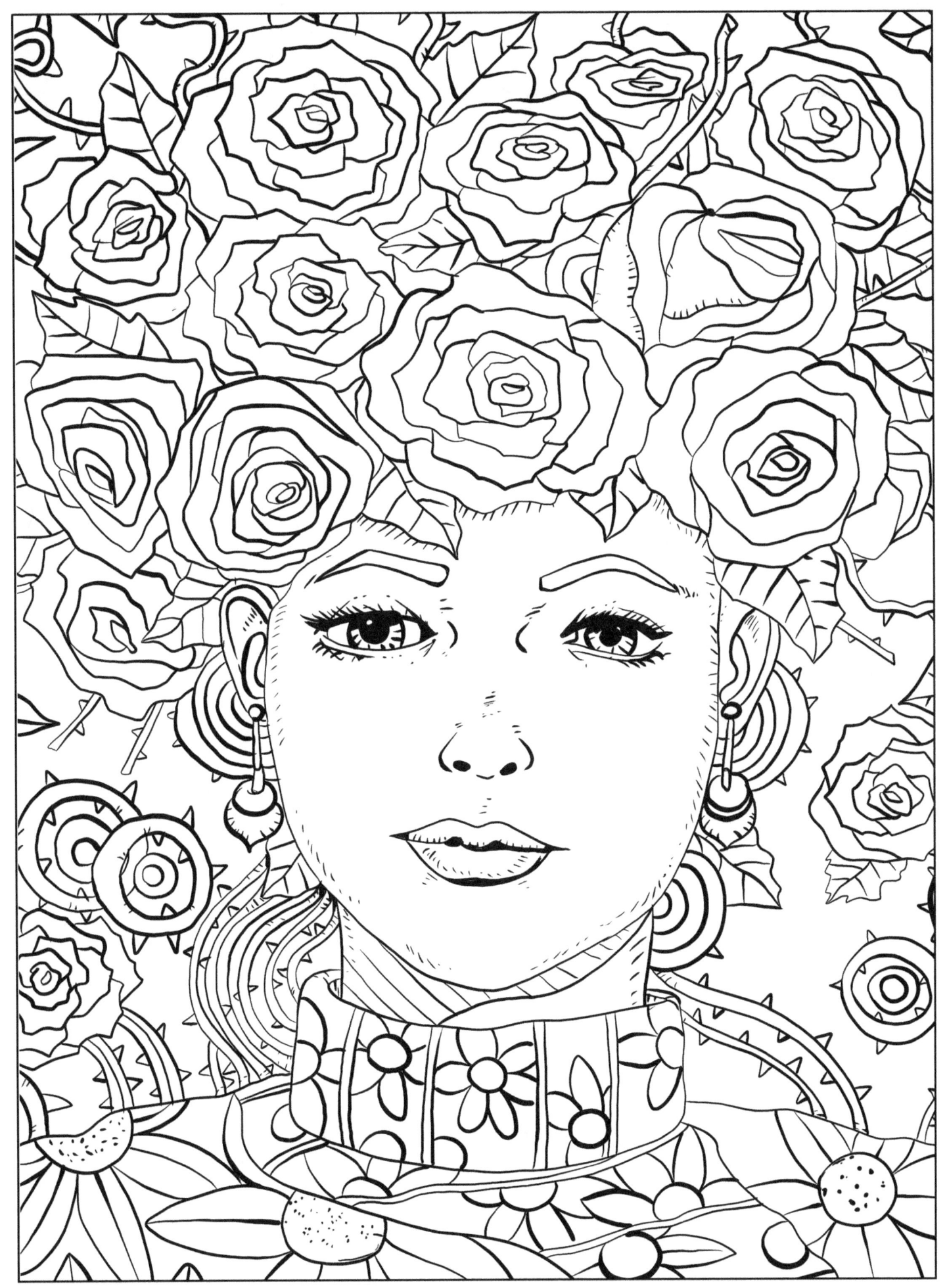

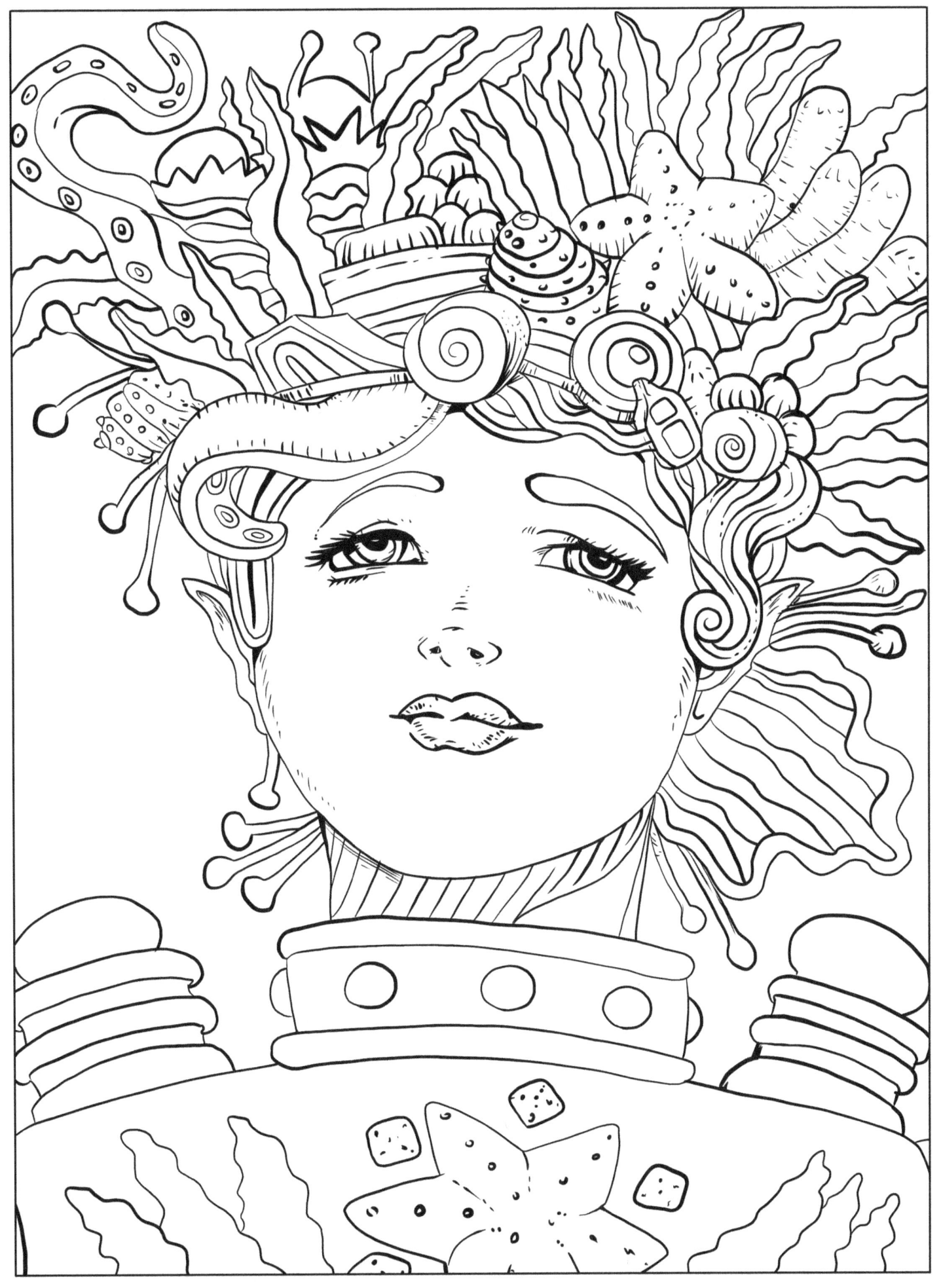

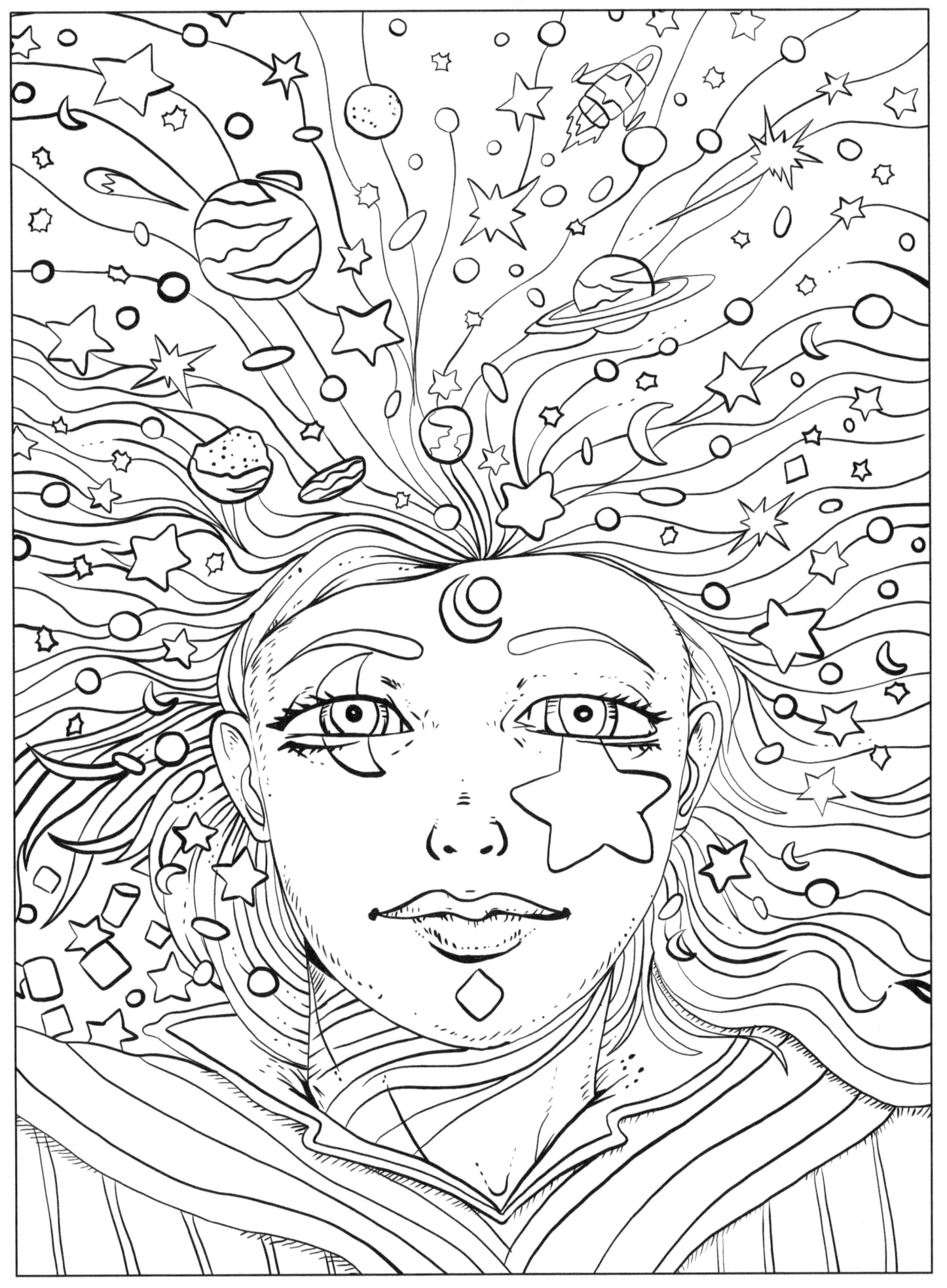

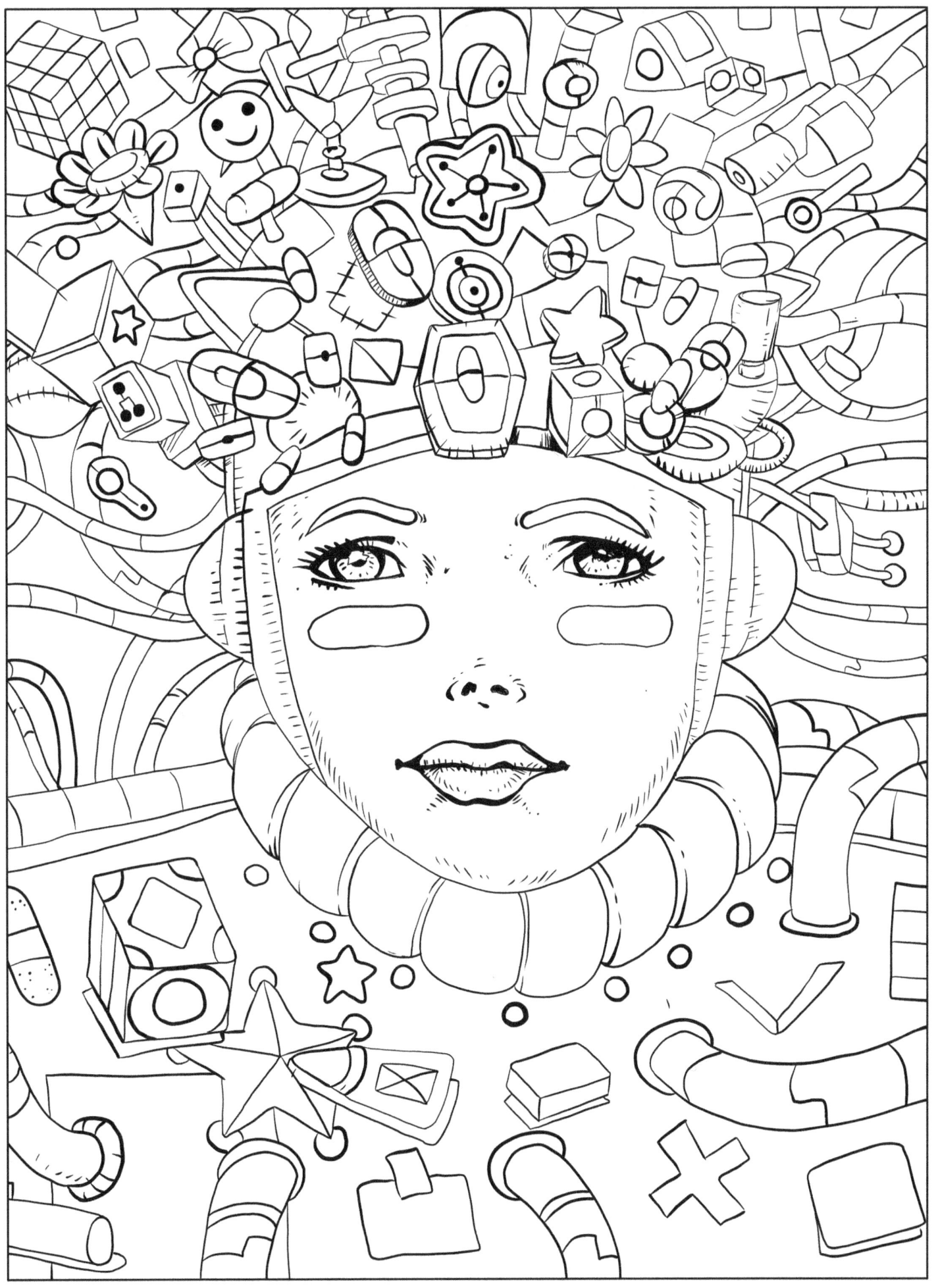

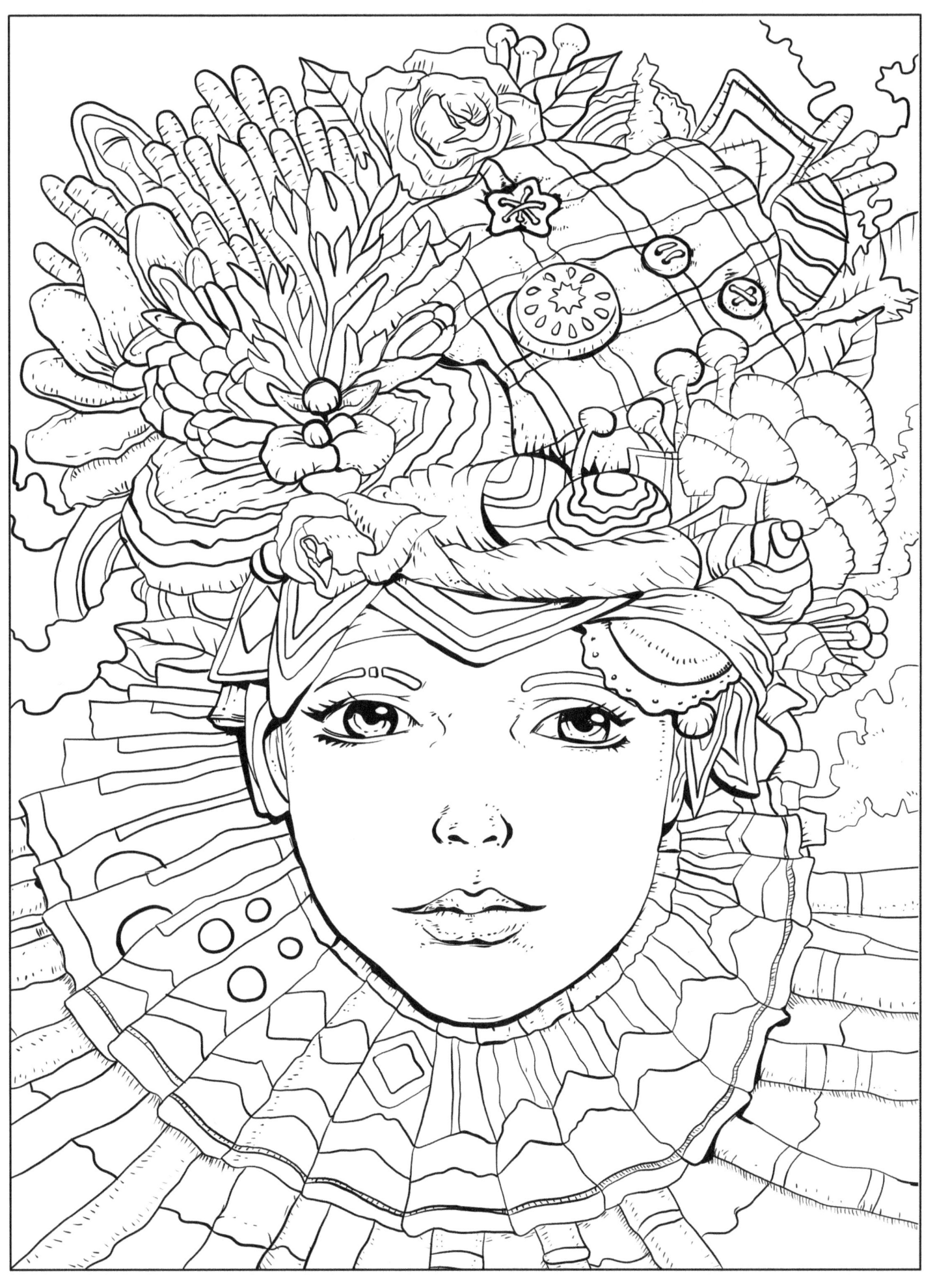

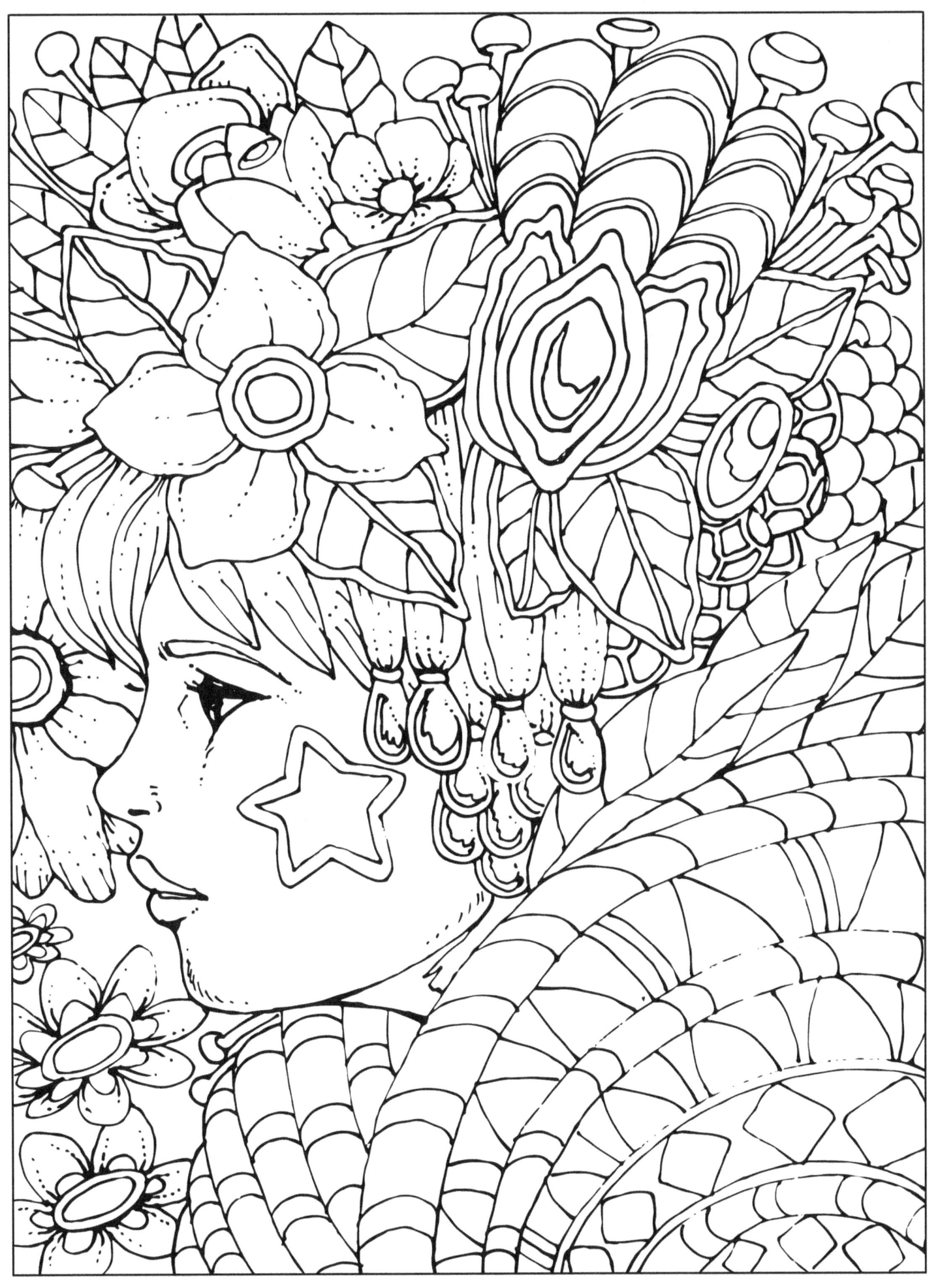

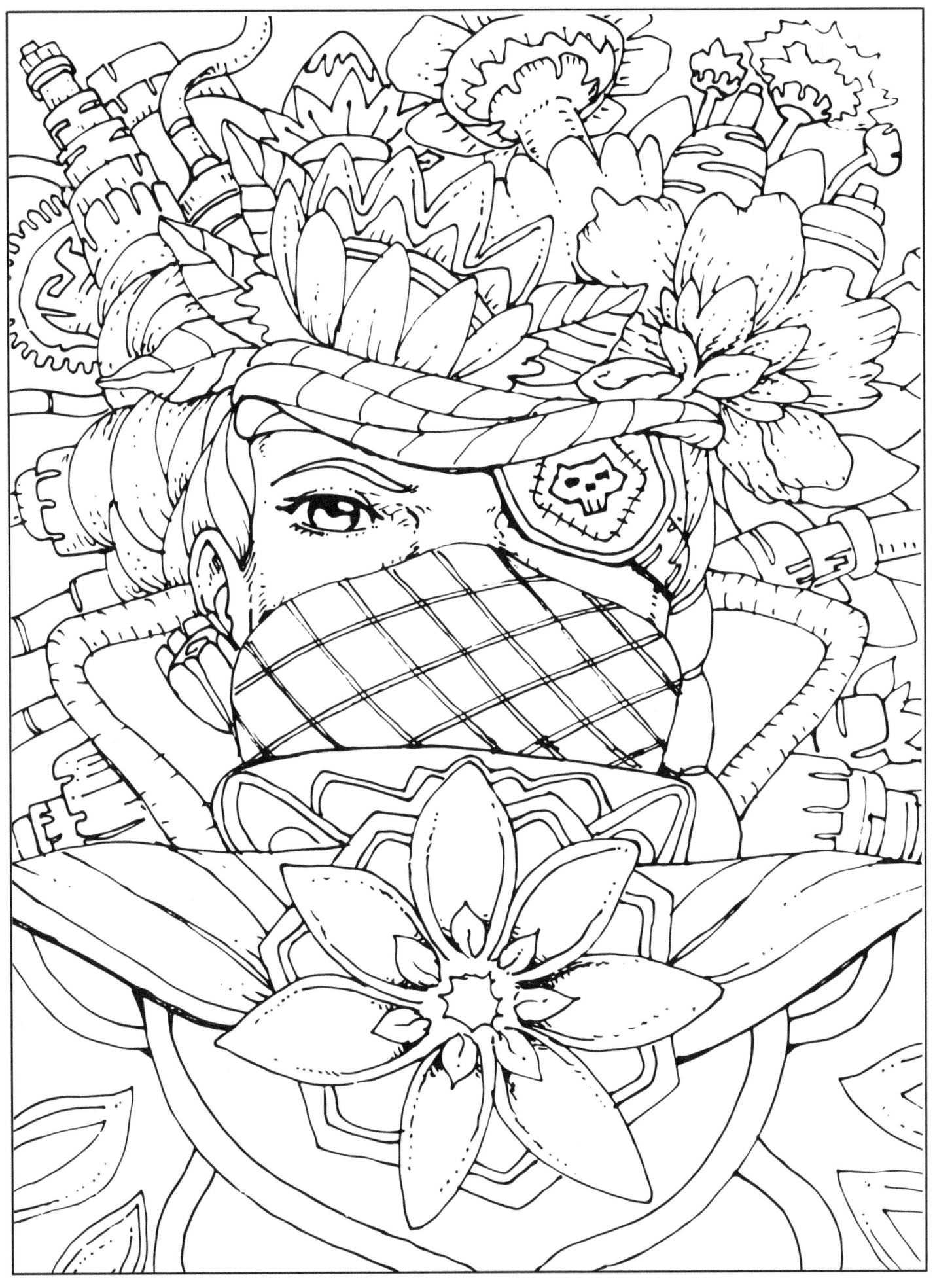

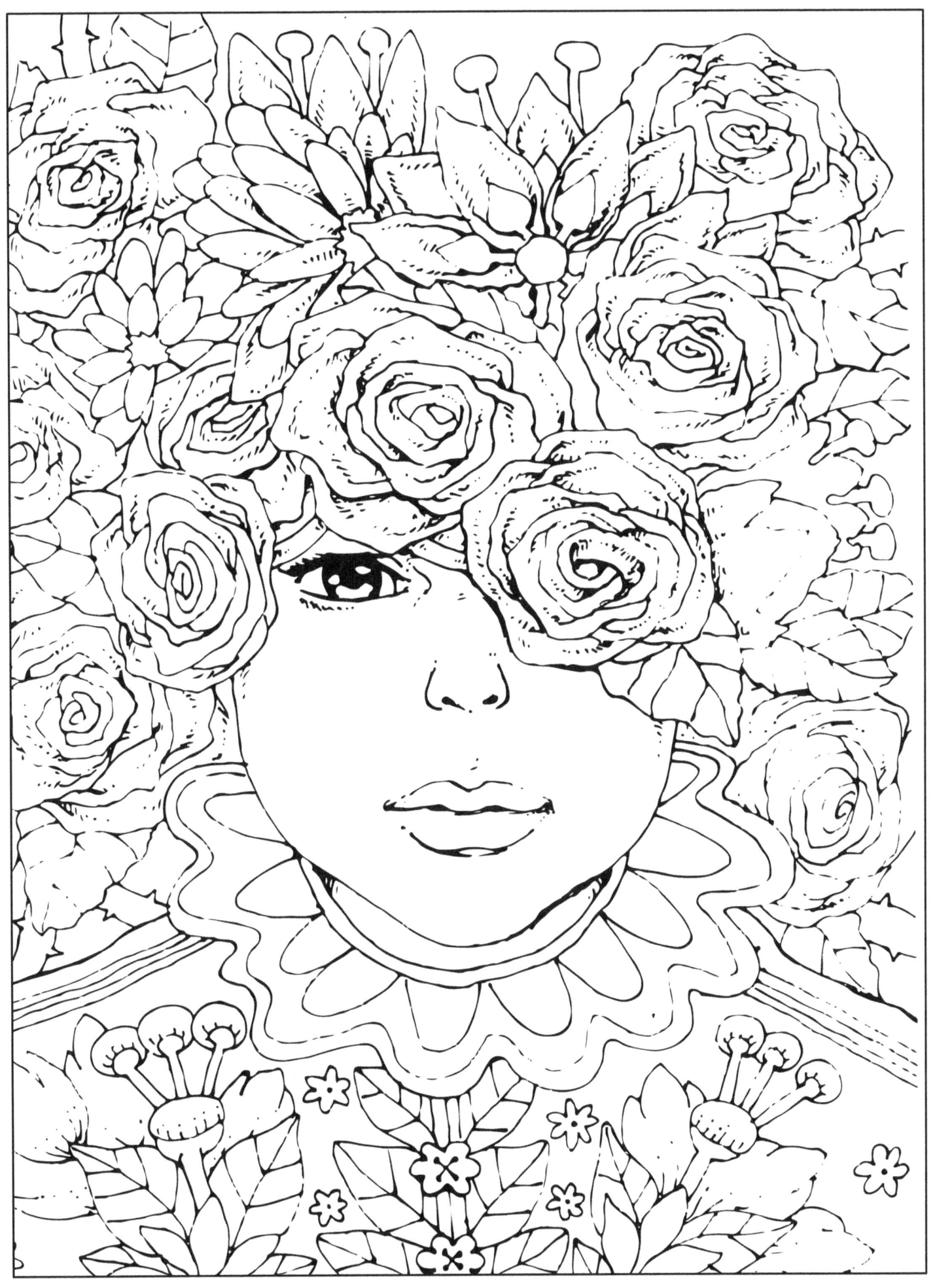

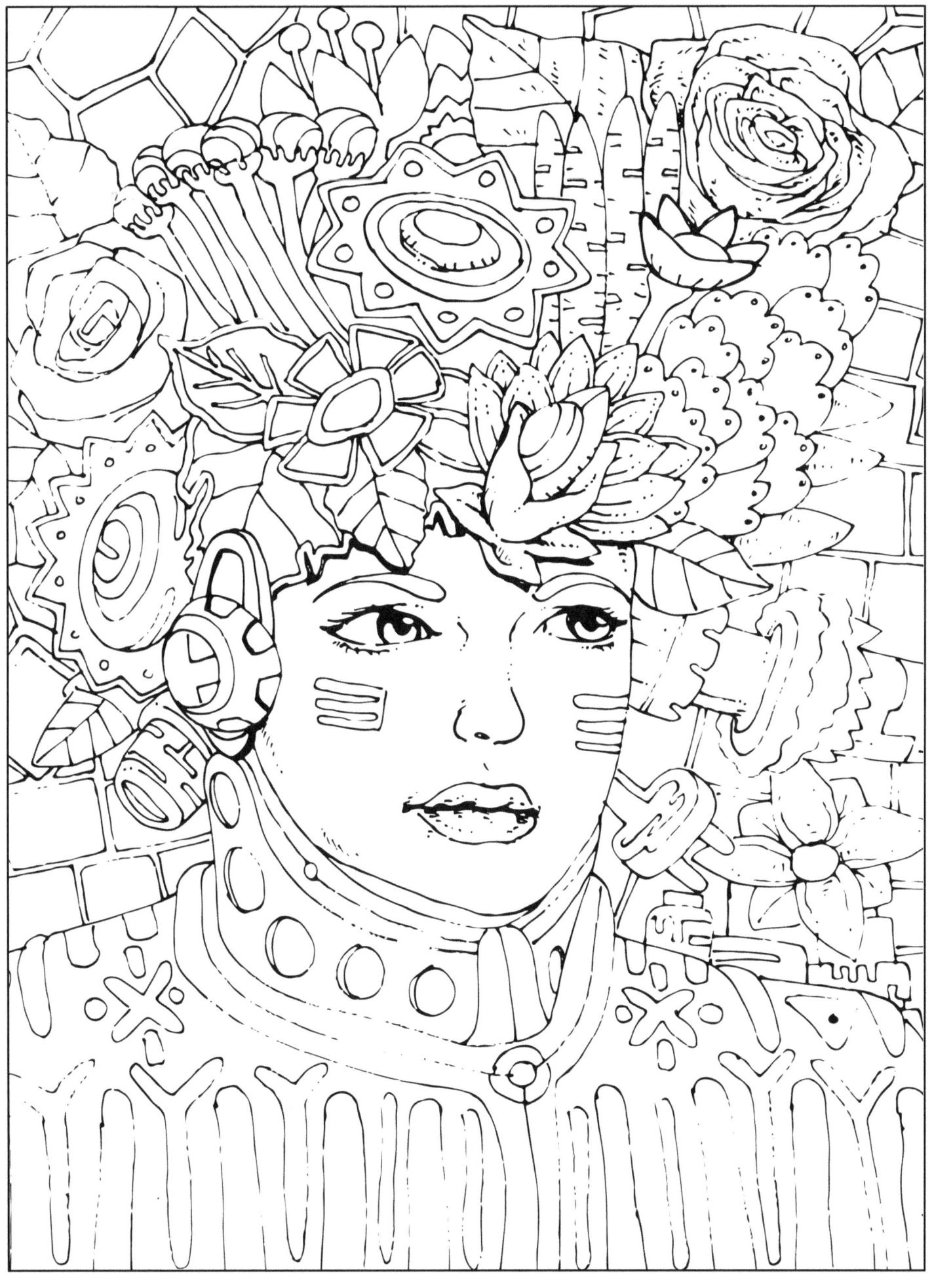

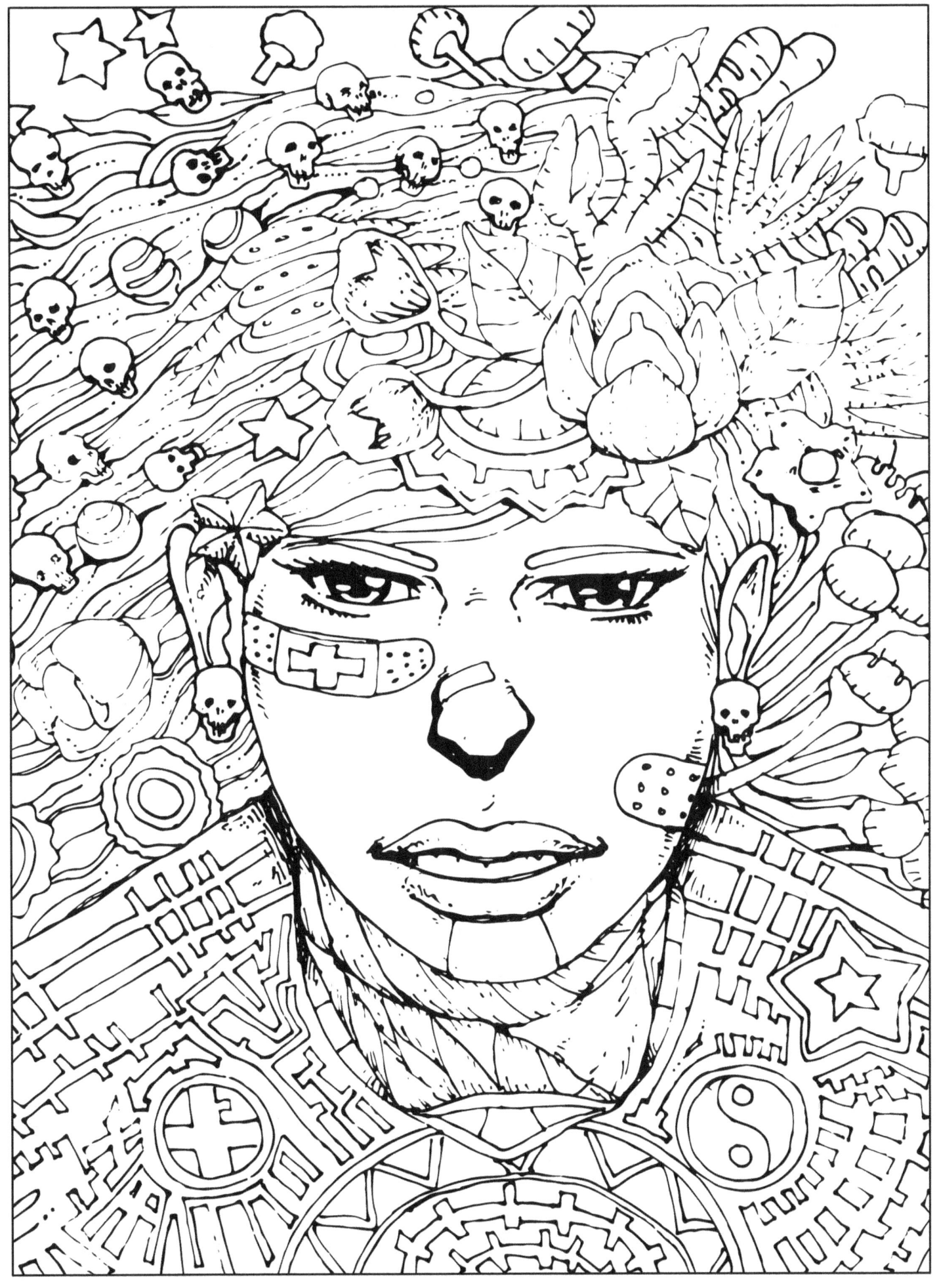

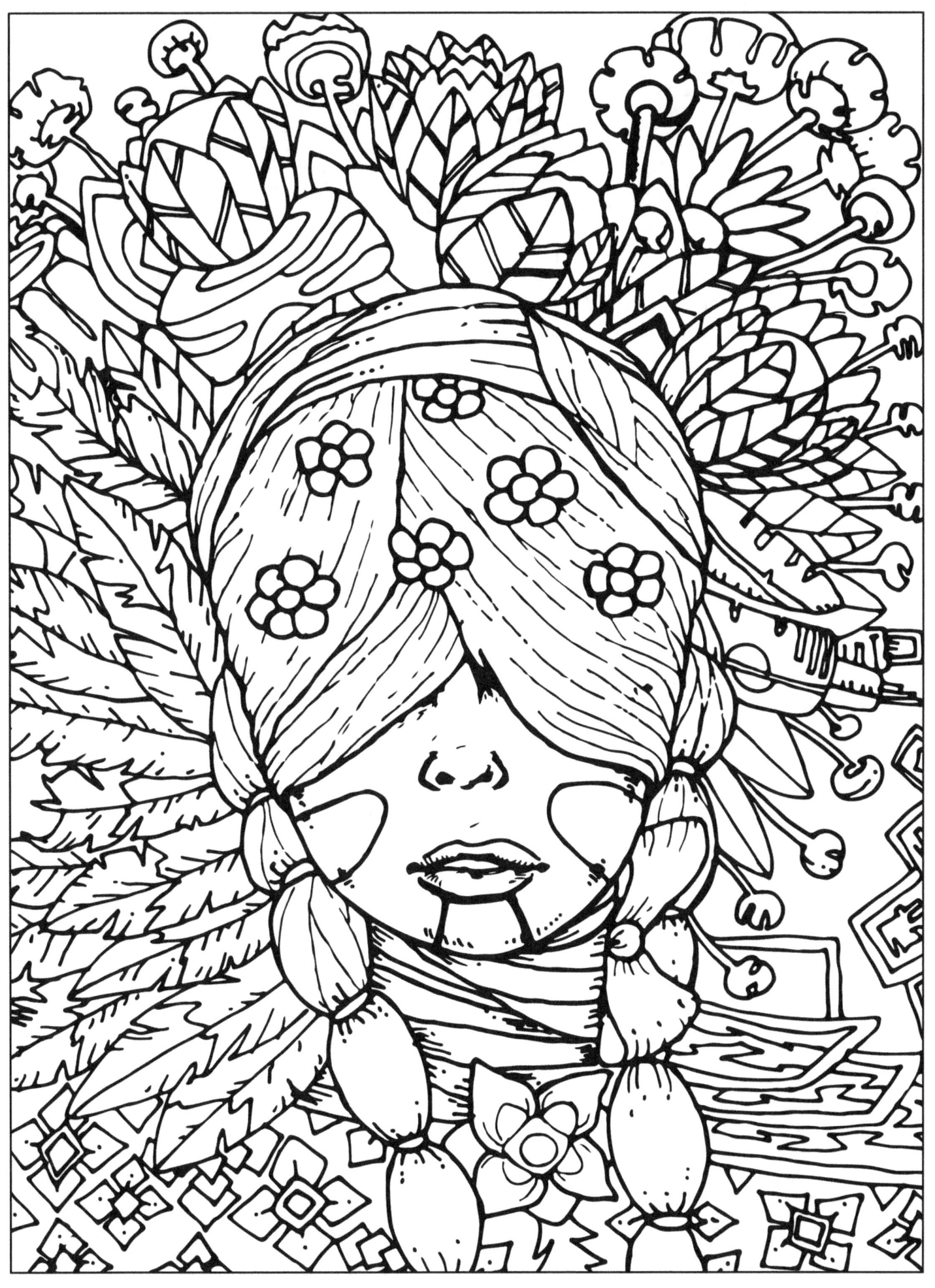

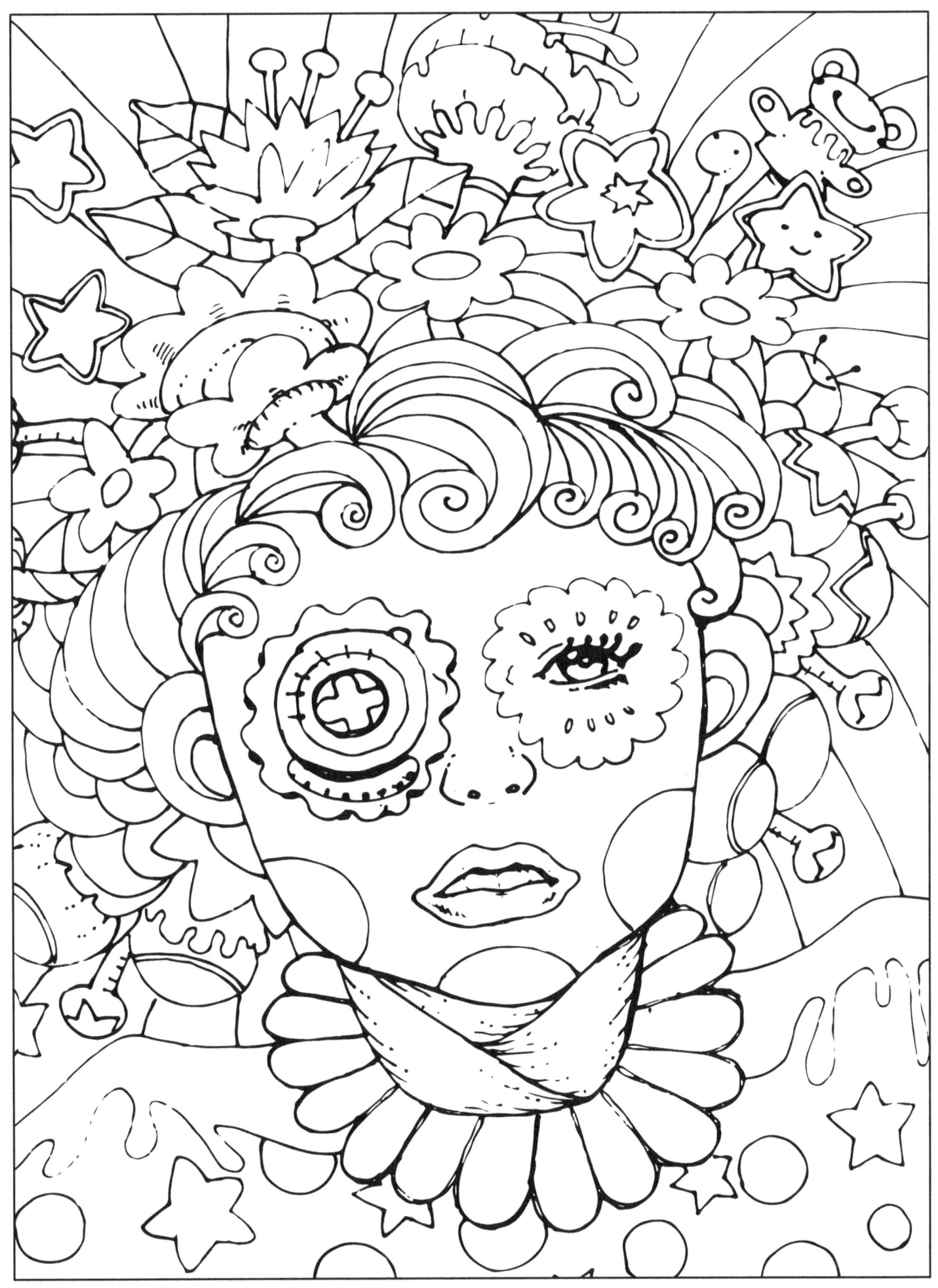

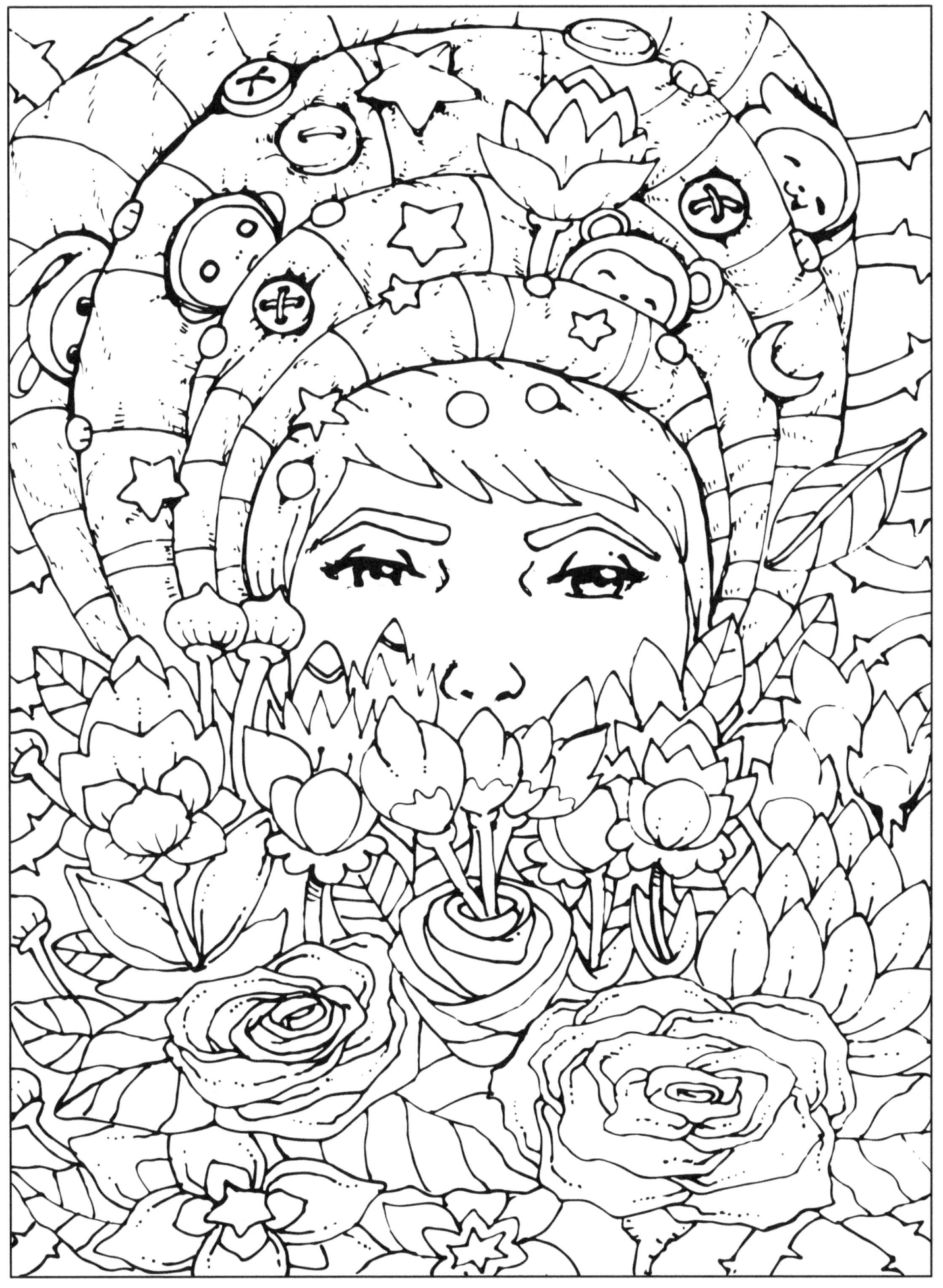

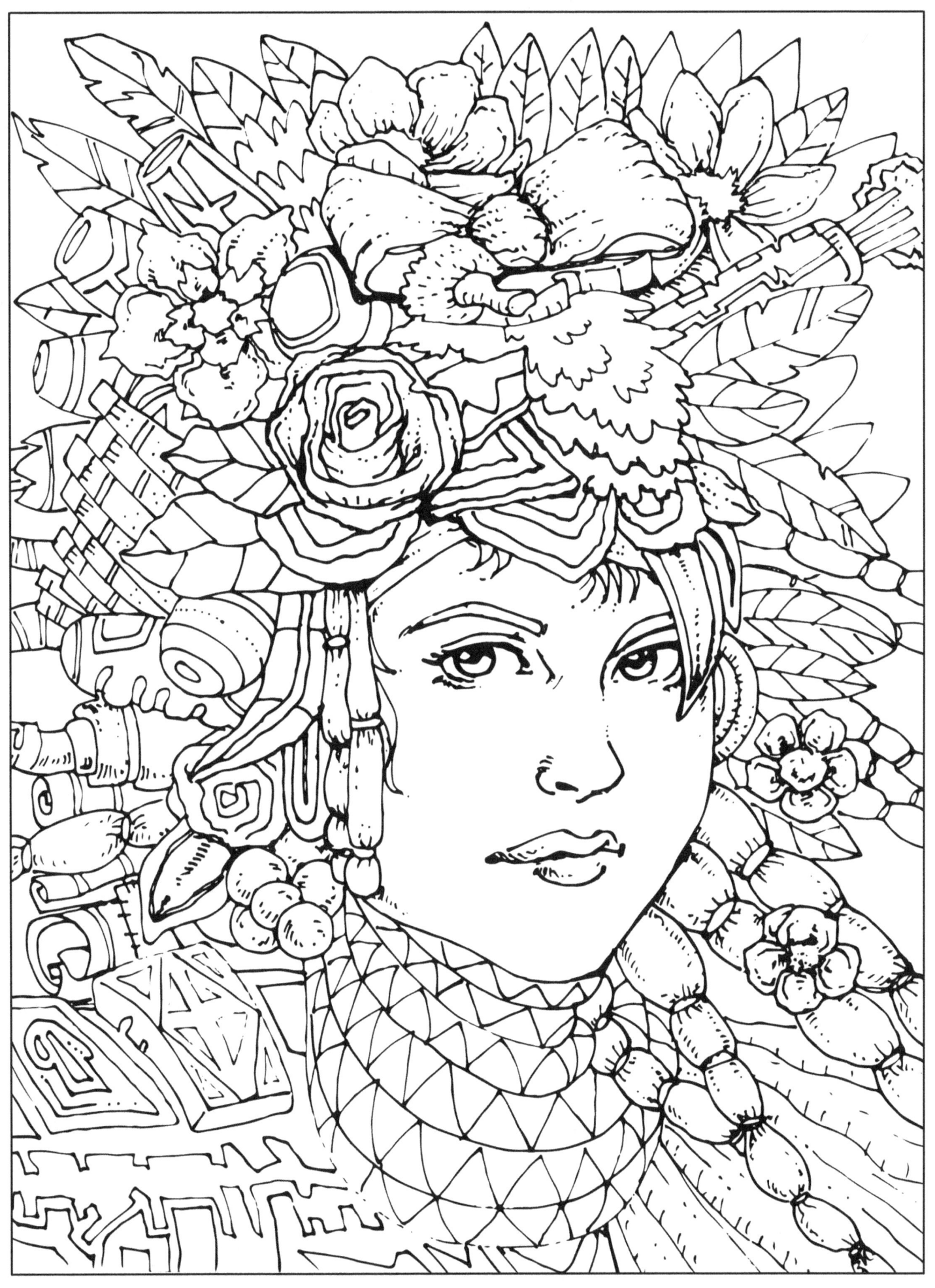

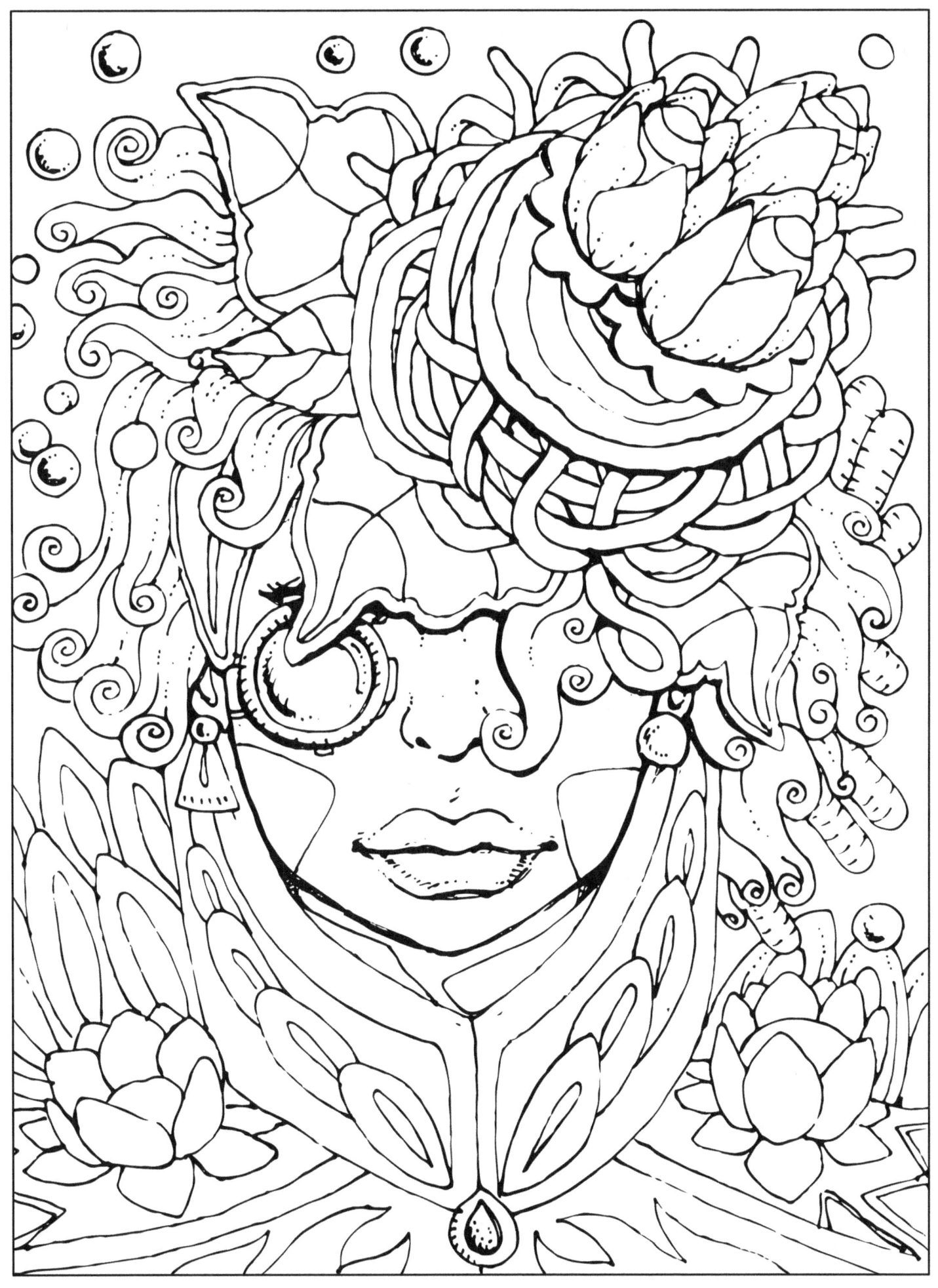

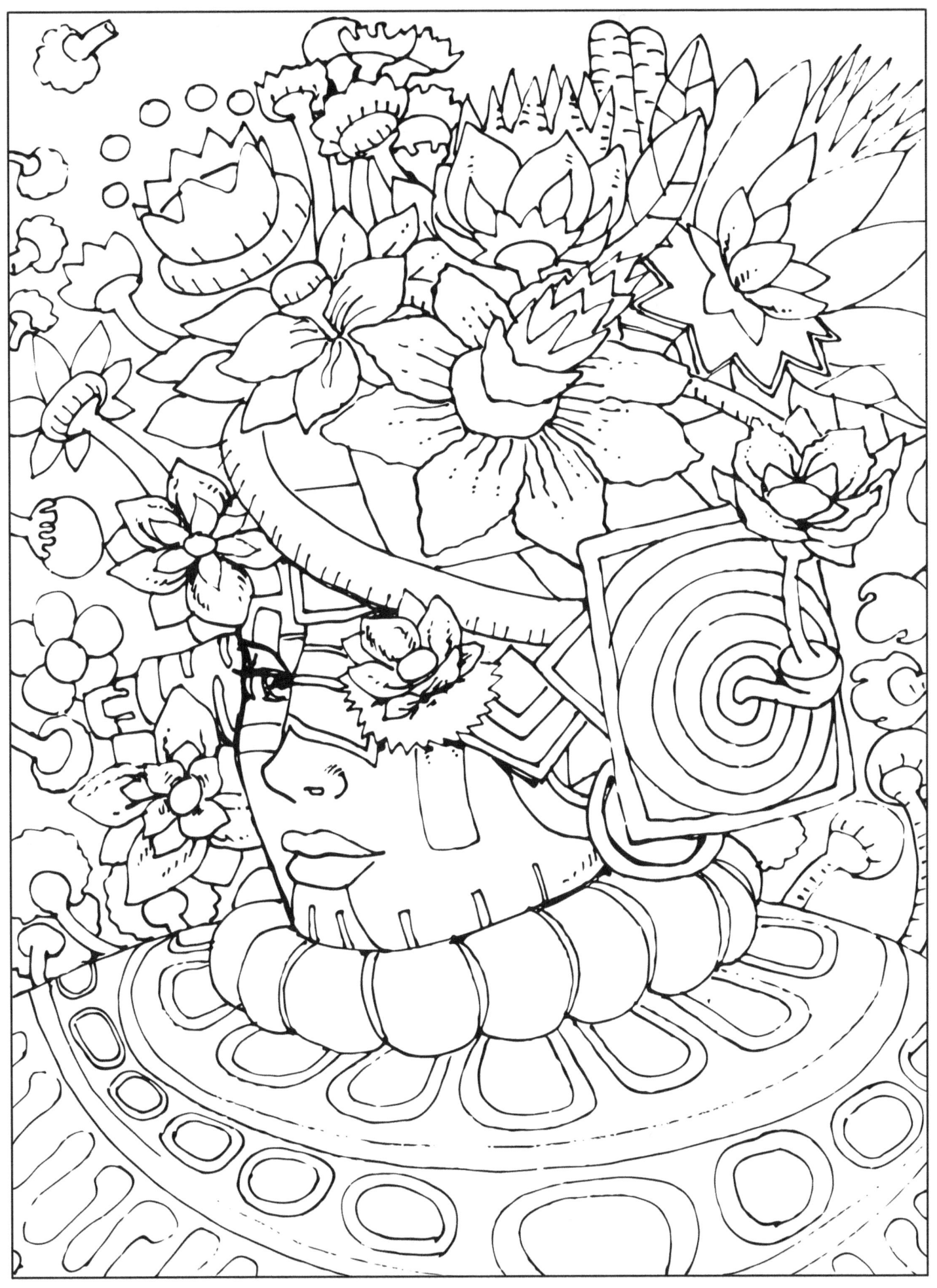

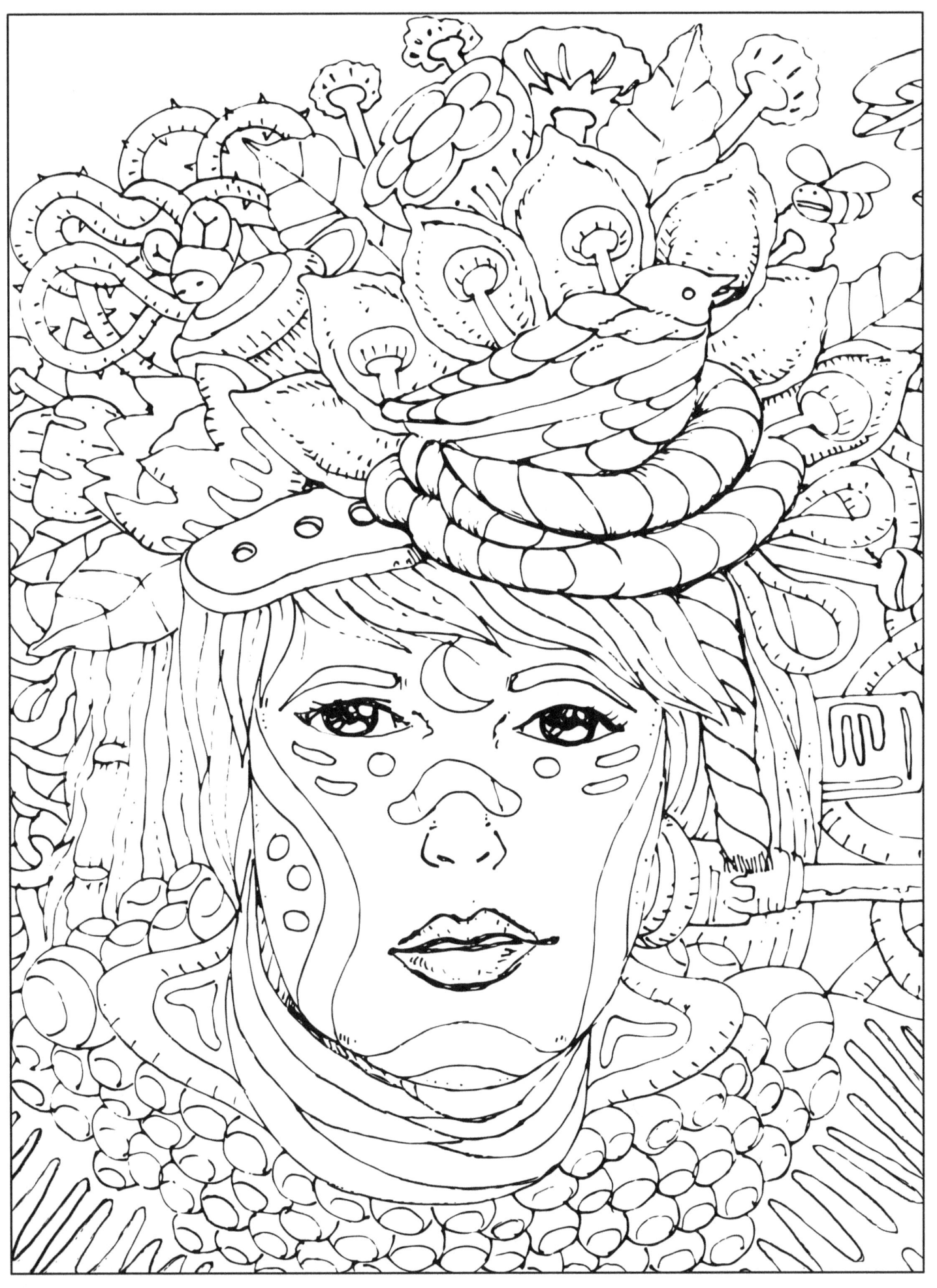

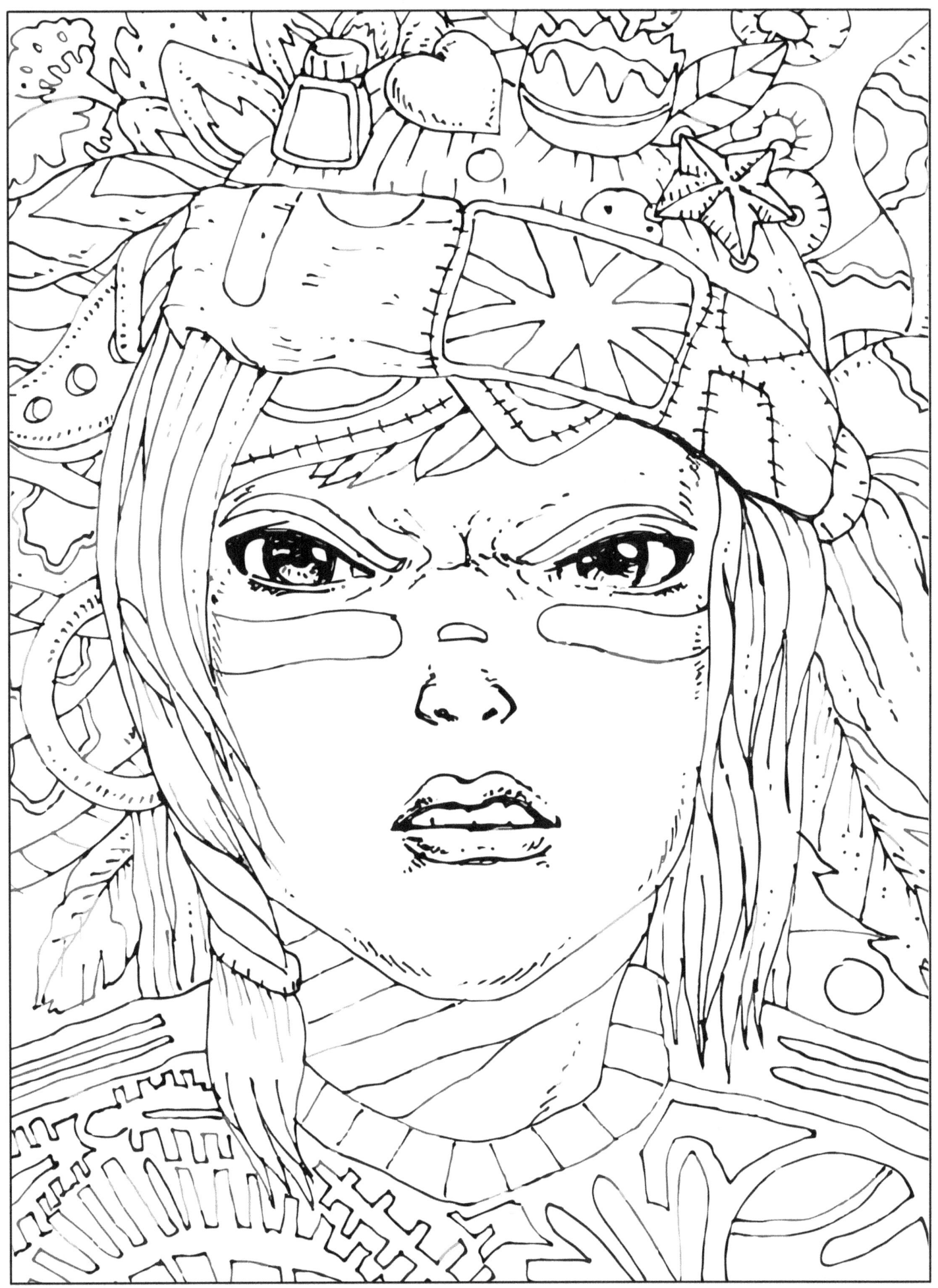

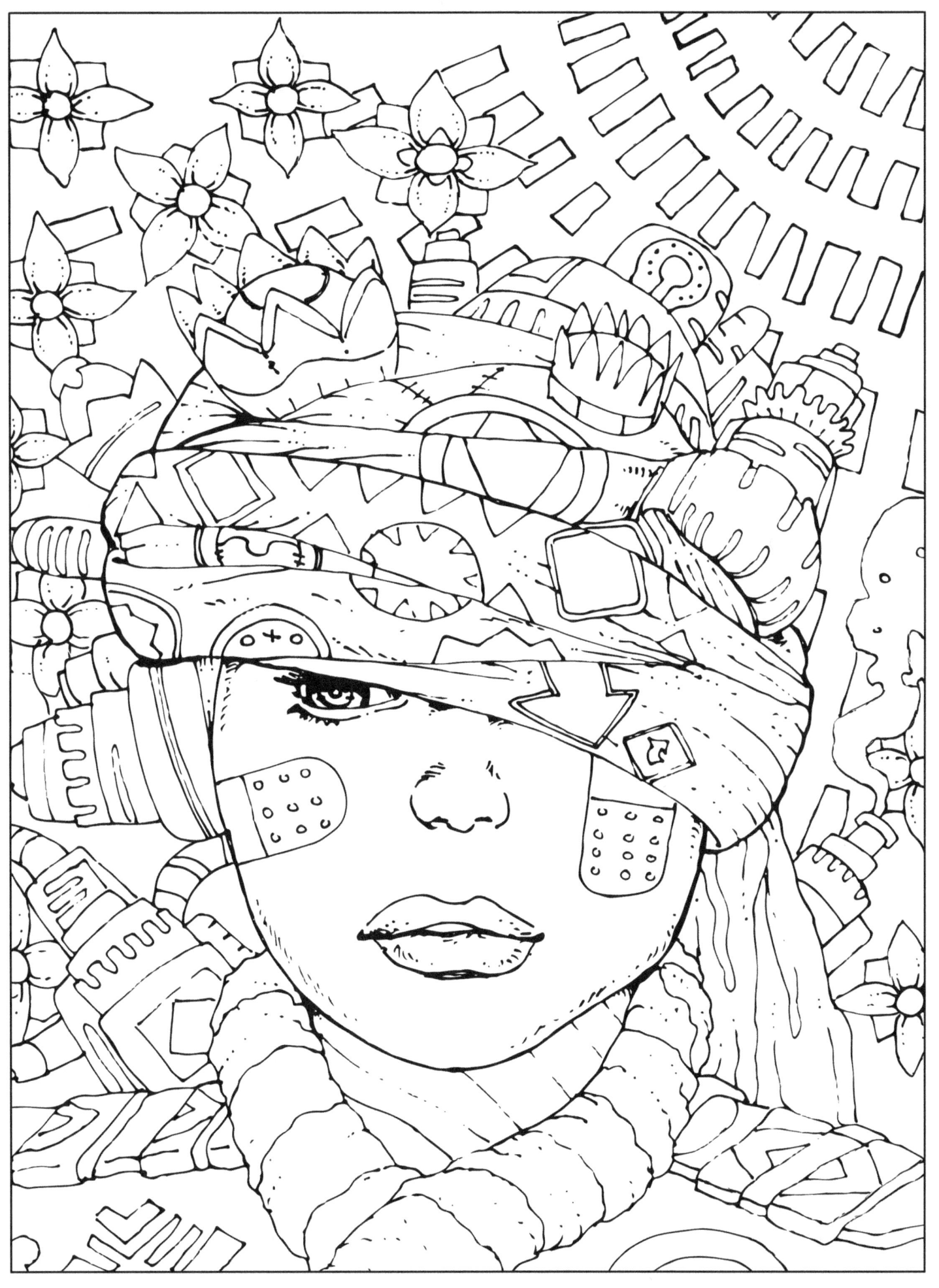

Thank you for supporting
ZenMaster Coloring Books!

I aim to make sure my customers have the most enjoyable and relaxing coloring experience possible and I would love to hear your feedback!

Please leave a review on Amazon and follow me on facebook for updates and free coloring pages!

https://www.facebook.com/zenmastercoloringbooks/

check out more of my books at:

amazon.com/author/zenmastercoloringbooks

Free Bonus Page!
from:

Happy Hour
Adult Coloring Book

https://amzn.com/1539662462

Also available in color by numbers!!

https://amzn.com/1976119944

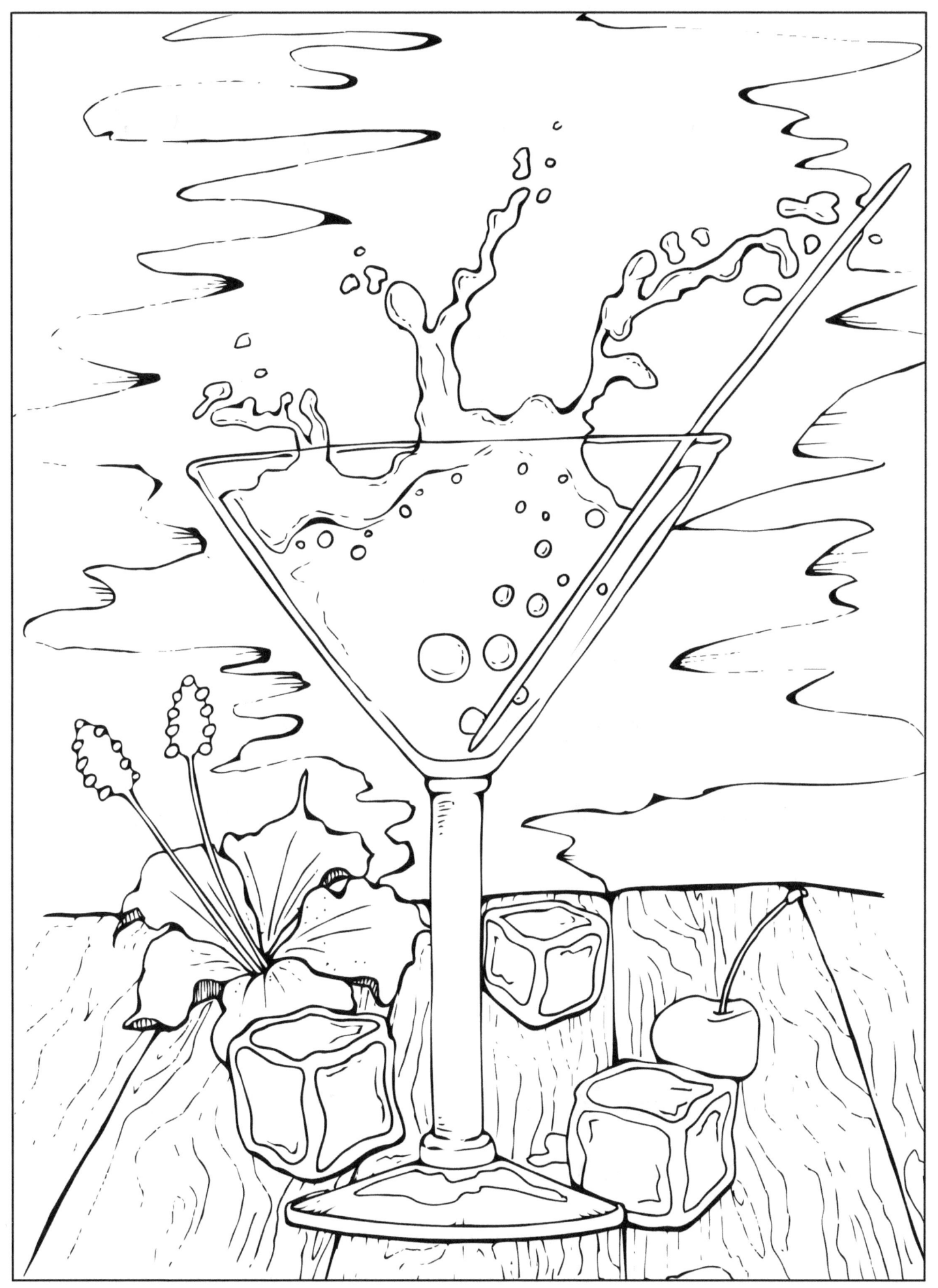

Free Bonus Page!
from:

Koi Fish

adult coloring book

https://amzn.com/1981470689

Also available in color by numbers!!
https://amzn.com/198149104X

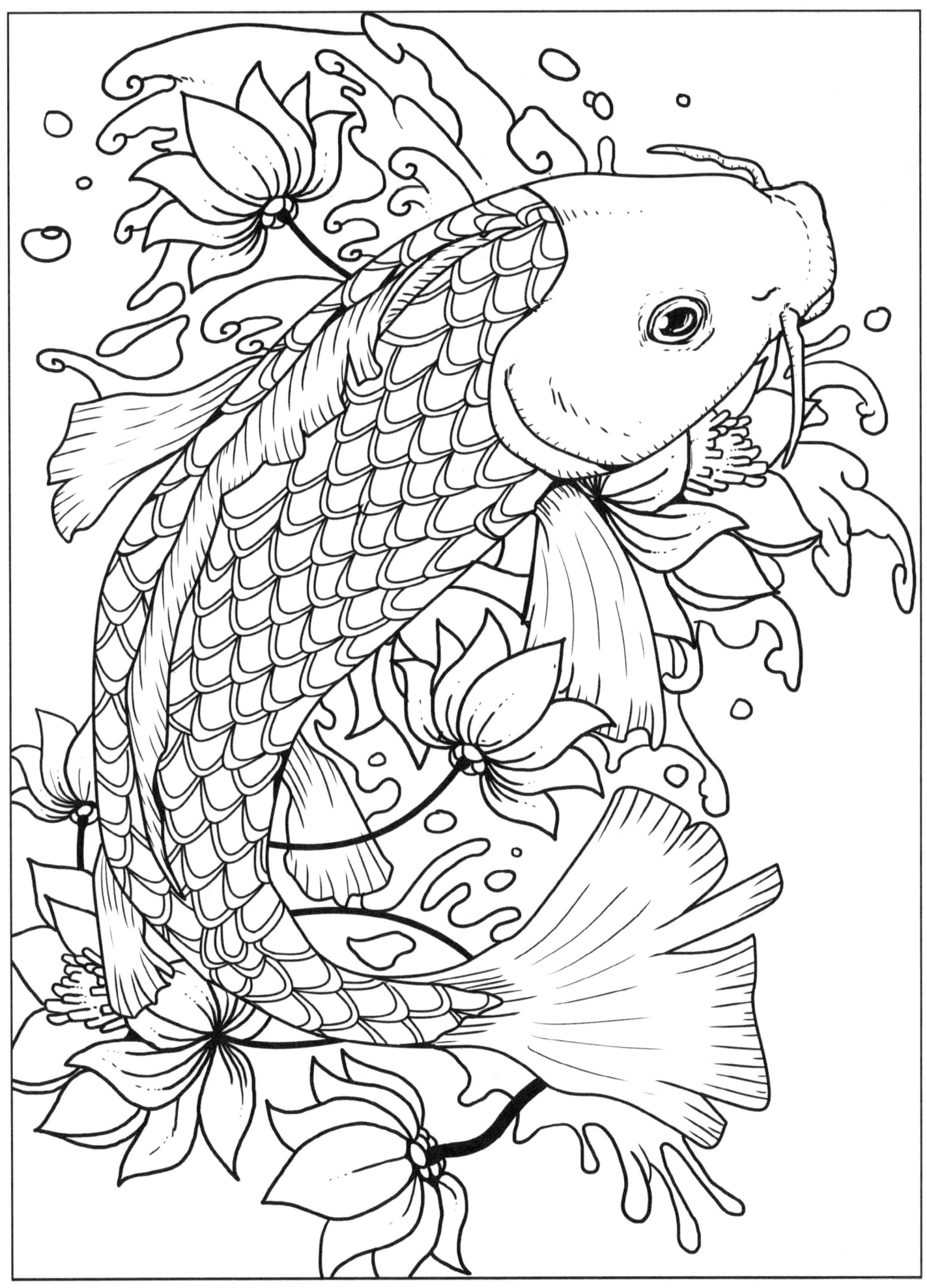

Free Bonus Page!
from:

YARN

coloring book for adults

https:/www.amzn.com/1079285059

Also available in color by numbers!!

https:/www.amzn.com/1079367241

And 5x8" Travel Size

https:/www.amzn.com/168741054

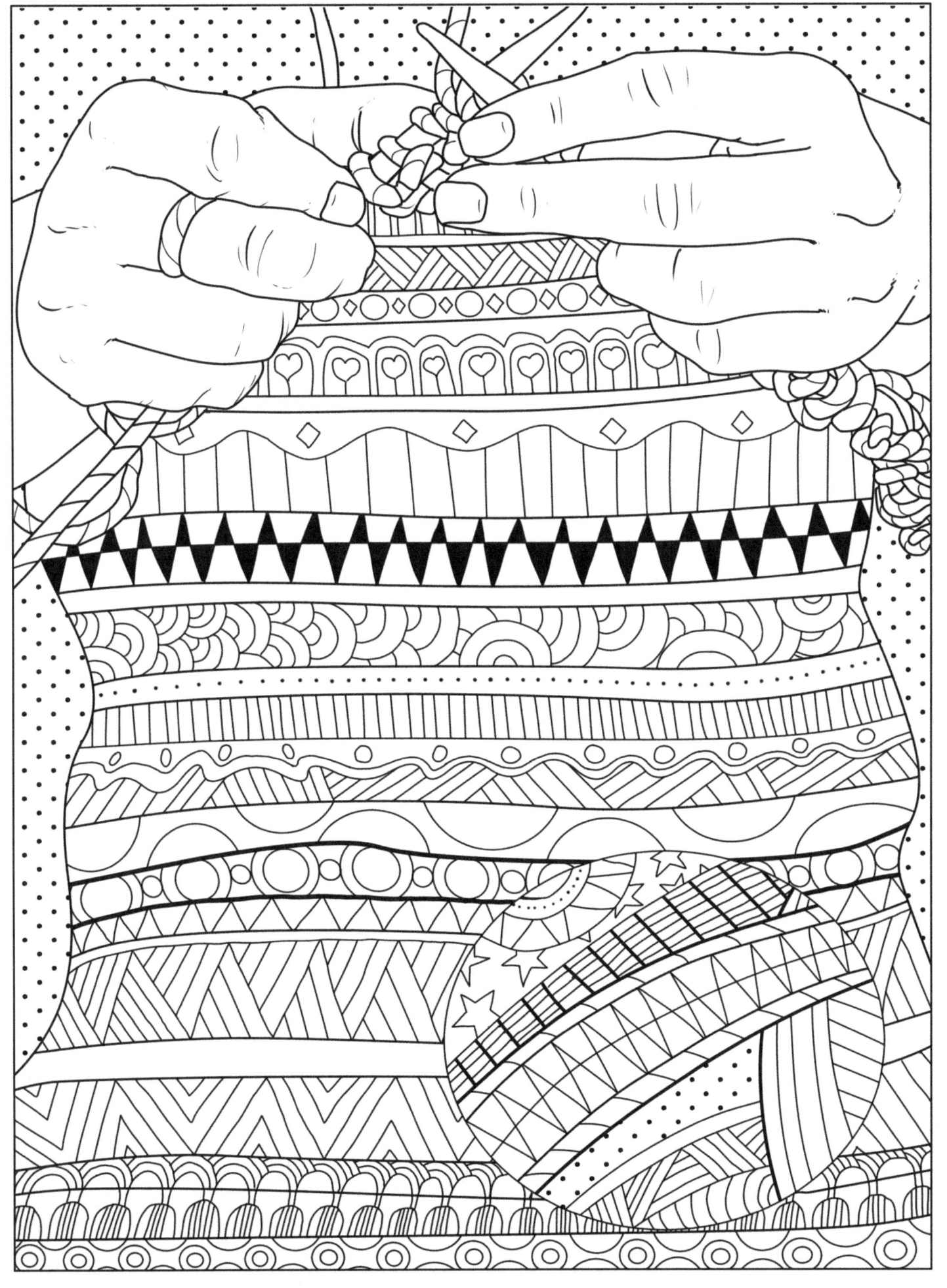